INSTANT
MIND POWER

The INSTANT-Series *Presents*

INSTANT

MIND POWER

How to Train and Sharpen Your Mental
Abilities Instantly!

Instant Series Publication

ISBN 978-1-516-84734-1

Printed in the United States of America

First Edition

FIRST STEP:

Before proceeding, visit http://www.instantseries.com, and join the **INSTANT Newsletter** now.

You will want to! :)

CONTENTS

Chapter 1:

A Human Super-Computer Upgrade

Warning, System Overload!

In today's digital age, our brains are completely *overwhelmed* by information saturation, and we all suffer difficulty every once in a while trying to sustain concentration for significant periods of time or trying to retain information.

Imagine how it must be for top-performing individuals, like business executives, politicians, and world leaders, who rely on having sharp minds all the time. Even they can suffer from such dysfunctions as *distractibility*, *fatigue*, *restlessness*, and *emotional breakdowns* once in a while.

We can't always control these dysfunctions and we can all agree that they wreak havoc on our everyday lives.

Thus, some people turn toward coffee or energy drinks to increase their efficiency, but those stimulants are just *Band-Aids*, providing **quick fixes**, not **long-term effectiveness**.

The truth is, there are very simple and beneficial ways to increase your <u>mental prowess</u>.

The Much-Needed Update

Everyone agrees that the **brain** is the most powerful tool that helps you not only achieve greatness, but also handle your daily life functions. It is a human super computer.

Having a positive mind is a wonderful thing, but being able to *optimize your brain activity* to achieve its greatest potential is even better.

There are countless advantages of <u>mind power</u>, such as:

1. Increased concentration
- Concentration is key to learning; for example, we understand theoretical concepts better when we listen to a lecturer explain them.

2. More awareness
- When you use the appropriate mind-boosting technique, you can retain information for longer periods of time.

3. Better memory
- Mind-boosting techniques can increase your memory potential, making you unstoppable! You'll be reaching all of your goals and objectives with ease.

Imagine what you could do with an optimized mind, where you have the ability to clear your mind of all unnecessary clutter and focus on what's most important.

Who wouldn't want to achieve this degree of concentration?

- Take this example, where you are a stay-at-home parent and the lifeblood of a household whose successful function depends on you. Your typical daily schedule includes grocery shopping, cleaning, and taking care of the children, amongst many other things. Some might say, *"That's easy."* But what they don't know is the degree to which you must be organized, and how if you forget to do just one of the many tasks you accomplish each day — the whole household is affected.

What is the solution to avoiding utter chaos and contributing the most to your family's well-being? The answer is **training your mind** to stay focused and alert at all times.

The <u>principle</u> here is that mind power is essential to reaching your goals successfully, even when doing the simplest things.

Exercise: Rewire Your Hardware

Before moving on to the next section, try to do the following exercise with any stopwatch at reach:

Below is a table with a series of numbers. Let's see if you can memorize the **bold numbers** (underlined) in less than **60 seconds**.

1	**2**	3	4	5	**6**	7	8
3	4	5	6	**7**	8	9	1
5	4	6	**7**	**9**	0	0	1

Follow the following guidelines:

1. First count only the numbers in **bold**.

2. Now, read all the numbers in the table *either* horizontally or vertically.

Now, something to ask yourself:

- By counting only the numbers in **bold** first … does *reading all the numbers* (horizontally or vertically) help you remember the bold numbers better? Did the bold numbers pop out more, not necessarily because they're bold, but because you've seen them before? Is it like trying to recall something you can't quite put your finger on, but once you do it becomes difficult to forget afterward, like a process of *slight familiarity* followed by *indirect reinforcement*?

The aim of this exercise is to show you how a certain **methodology** can *indirectly* but *automatically* help you register, reinforce, and retain information better; hence, a **simple intended action** of "*reading all the numbers horizontally or vertically*" has an **added unintended effect** of "*reinforcing the bold numbers in your mind.*"

How's that for mind hacking (without you even noticing)?

By training your mind, you can come up with creative loopholes to hack your own mind to get things done easier and simplify your life.

Now, let's move on for more insights on mental-enhancing methods.

Chapter 2:

Program Your Mind to Get Things Done

Mental Numbing

Distraction is one of the biggest threats to **concentration**. Unfortunately, it happens more often than not and takes on many different forms, such as emergencies, interruptions, and even social media — the biggest time devourer of them all!

Unless you have been gifted with solid focusing skills, you aren't immune to the predator that distraction can be. It's like a hunting lion and you are its buffalo. It lures you away from your group (a focal point), and without the proper faculties to outsmart this predator, you're doomed.

So how do you develop mind power and increase your concentration?

One solution to this ever-growing problem is a technique we like to call "**mental numbing.**" Mental numbing suppresses your sensitivity to nonessential stimuli, allowing you to remain focused on what is most important to you at that moment. When using this technique you are in an almost robotic state, programmed for a specific task.

Mental numbing actually trains your mind to *block out* any type of distraction. It draws upon a "**horizontal mind map**" of your object of focus — projects, written content, routines, programs, objectives, or whatever object needs your complete concentration — and numbs you from all outside emotions or sensations.

Horizontal Mind Mapping

Let's explain and go through the **mental numbing** and **horizontal mind mapping** processes *step-by-step*.

In order for you to be focused on one thing (and one thing only), you have to be able to ignore the rest. But first you have to know what your focus needs to be on, right?

This is when horizontal mind mapping comes in handy. It consists of writing down a "**code of conduct**" or a *set of instructions* that your brain needs to follow in the exact order it's written in to achieve focus. (Think of it like a **mind oath**.)

Horizontal mind mapping conditions your mind to follow the path after you've registered it. When the mind is conditioned by a rule or an instruction, you are numbing it to concentrate on that one rule and block out anything outside of that objective (i.e. distraction) until it reaches the next rule, and all the way to the final point of the instruction, or your satisfying "end goal."

For example, it's similar to the training process for a mechanic: If they don't follow the instructions for installing a carburetor to a "T," they will incorrectly install it and fail.

When creating a horizontal mind map, the conditions your mind has to follow should be:

- Ranked in order of importance

- Interrelated

- Written horizontally

Mapping Scenarios

Take this example, where you are a teacher who's grading assignments that could give students a shot at being accepted into the most prestigious college in the country.

You must do your best to remain focused on only those students who have the most accurate answers.

But...

What about those students whose answers are almost right? You know that they understand the material, but they just have a difficult time explaining their answers. What if you regret your decision for not giving them more points? These types of questions can distract you from making the right decisions.

For your mind to be focused on the bare bones essential, boost your concentration through mental numbing, in which your horizontal mind map will condition your brain to choose the students with the best answers.

As this teacher, your <u>horizontal mind map</u> could look something like this:

- Crucial assignment / Assignment for most prestigious college's admission / Answers must be the most accurate / Only students with the most accurate answers can receive the maximum amount of points

All of these conditions tell you exactly what to do so you stay on course and are automatically numb to any distractions, such as interpreting what you think the students meant so that they can pass their exam, or feeling sorry for a student who you think deserved a second chance.

Another example: Let's say the U.S. ambassador to France has to decide what to do about a child who's been declared an American but was born in France to a French citizen.

Having seen the files and pictures of the child's American sibling, his staff realizes that the child bares a striking resemblance to his sibling, and so, obviously, there is no question about the child's citizenry. But the ambassador ignores his staff's comments and orders a DNA test anyway.

Because he is completely focused on what matters most and blocks out his staff's comments and the photographic evidence, the ambassador is able to show absolute neutrality in his final decision about the child.

Here's his possible <u>horizontal mind map</u>:

- Child born abroad to one parent who's a non-U.S. citizen / Photographic evidence or paperwork not enough / DNA testing necessary

Here is **one last example** of a beauty pageant judge mental numbing in their decision making. A judge's smile can be very misleading to candidates, but a non-emotional straight face can really freak contestants out!

The beauty pageant judge's <u>horizontal mind map</u> would look something like this:

- Pageant queen / Should be well-spoken / Should be imperturbable / Deserves the title

In both examples, the ambassador and the judge had absolute mind power by blocking out non-essential emotions and stimuli.

In summary, by blocking out distractions…

1. You can concentrate on one task at a time.

2. You work faster.

3. You reach goals quicker.

Remember, for mental numbing to work you must draw a horizontal mind map first, then follow it to a "T."

Exercise: Create Horizontal Mind Maps

Let's practice with the following exercise:

1.) Everybody needs to concentrate, but some people need to do it more than others. What would be the appropriate horizontal mind map for:

- train driver

- airplane pilot

- high school teacher (12th grade)

- writer

Be as accurate as you can. Here's an example to get you started: A news anchor's horizontal mind map would look like this:

- Be as neutral as possible / Transmit accurate and verified information to the public / Concentrate on the information that is being transmitted / Stay focused and professional at all times

2.) Can this method make some of the professionals listed above work faster and more effectively? Why or why not?

Chapter 3:

Hack Your Mind to Retrieve Information

Outdated Repetition

Elementary school students often use **repetition** to memorize a poem or their multiplication tables. It's an exhausting process, but the information is simple and straightforward, and children want to gain the teacher's approval (at least most of them), so they're happy to repeat something all day long, over and over again, until they know it by heart.

But as we grow older, the content becomes harder and the poems longer, and learning things by rote isn't always the easiest method. Not only do we need to memorize information, but we also need to understand it and retain it for longer periods of time.

Using repetition to your advantage is not just about repeating the same information over and over again, it's also about harmonizing the action of repetition with how the mind really stores information, particularly when it come to a complex task or large amount of written content.

Mind power should not only be about training your brain to work in a certain way, but it should also be about devising ways to trick it into being more effective, *aka* **mind hacking**.

- For example, each one of us likes to organize our time and space so that working is more pleasant and we are more productive at our jobs. But how successful are we really at creating the right environment for such mental activity? Instead, we cut corners: starting an hour late, taking too many breaks, or putting something off until tomorrow.

Updated Repetition

So how do we use repetition to boost our mind, in turn boosting our productivity?

The answer is simple, but maybe not so obvious: by reproducing the **same exact situation** each time you are going through a routine or reading content. Recreate the same smells, the same body movements, the same location, etc.

Mentally record your repetition like a **movie scene** to be stored in your head.

- For example, if you are resting your chin on your hand while studying written content, you should repeat that motion every time you read that piece of writing. Or, if you are learning a dance routine and you are supposed to snap your fingers on a certain beat, you should repeat that same behavior every time you practice the routine.

The mind can remember content, but sometimes it needs help recovering it.

So if you create the same environment (the positioning of your books, the set-up of your desk, the smell of a burning incense stick, etc.) every time you study the content, then you can train your mind to revisit that instance whenever you need to retrieve the information, say for a test or a presentation.

Don't think of it as repetition; think of it as recording a movie scene.

It's like your mind is a secret passage that leads to a chamber (the stored content). And the only way through the passage is by using a secret code (the environment you've re-created every time). It's like, the information is right there, and, yet, you can't get to it…until now.

Imagine the possibilities when applying this simple method.

Exercise: System Recovery Mode

Here's an assignment for you:

From now on, whenever you wish to memorize written content, a routine, a recommendation, or instructions, create an environment that you can repeat each and every time.

Feel free to introduce elements such as music, candles, even a distinct painting — whatever will help you feel comfortable.

- Do you get more and more comfortable each time you go through your training session? Does using mind power get easier over time?

Chapter 4:

Rewrite Your Mind to Channel Your Thoughts

Control Over Your Mind

Have you ever read a great book and wondered how the author was able to come up with such an extraordinary story?

Take, for example, the 19th-century Russian novelist **Fyodor Dostoevsky,** who captivates readers with his accurate description of the human condition; or the ancient Greek author **Homer** whose tales, *The Iliad* and *The*

Odyssey, have been told numerous times over centuries and still fascinate readers.

How did they do it?

Some people might think that these authors were under the influence of some kind of powerful drug because there is no way they were that inspired or had that big of an imagination.

But, actually, the <u>answer</u> is quite simple: If you want to produce great ideas, you **must order your mind** to write them. Most of the time, it's not a lack of inspiration that prevents you from coming up with these ideas, rather, it's a lack of *time* and *energy*.

What does writing have to do with mind power?

Most of the time we think we are in control of our mind, but it's the mind that is in control of us (e.g., succumbing to bad habits, quitting because you don't "feel like it," etc.), and to become commander again you must hijack your mind and imprison these **little voices** in your head.

Writing is a great way to practice control and to focus your limitless thoughts.

The mind works at its best and is most stimulated when used in conjunction with writing. And once you start writing, sometimes it's near impossible to stop until you are completely satisfied with what you've written. (See, it has nothing to do with anything you can ingest or inhale, so stop trying to get prescriptions for Provigil or Adderall when you don't need to!)

Loading Mental Data

This is how it works: Suppose you are assigned to write an article for a magazine about race cars. But you have no prior knowledge of race cars and have never even watched an auto race.

What do you do?

Well, you might try Googling the term "race car." But maybe your search isn't providing the right information that you need.

Now what? How do you come up with great content about race cars?

1. Start by writing "race cars" on your screen (or paper).

2. Stimulate your mind by reading the phrase a couple times.

3. Then start writing down any ideas that come to mind and continue to add to the list.

Here's what it might look like if someone were to use this method to write about race cars:

Start with a title: Race Cars

Add a few ideas: Intense speed, risky but adrenaline rush, pays good money...

(Write down about five main ideas. These will serve as keywords in your text.)

Introduce your content: "Race cars have always been live-action seekers' favorite sport..."

Good content has to captivate its readers. So it's not always so much about being an expert on the subject, but, rather, it's about how you present the content so that it will keep your readers interested.

Instant Configuration

The *race car example* is a bit more formal, but what if you only need to write a simple note or jot down a few lines for a quick, unexpected speech?

You don't need keywords, but you do need to **snap your brain** to do it. This is **instant configuration**. (Think of it as being a computer, and you have to adjust the settings before each thing you do.)

With this, you configure your brain to write exactly what it is you need it to, like a *sick note* to your boss, or a *thank-you note* to your child's teacher.

Instant configuration of the mind leads to instant concentration, like a sudden jolt of unexpected shock that wakes you up and boosts your brain immediately, allowing you to write excellent content in a short period of time (5, 10, or 20 minutes). You will have a continuous flow of ideas until you are absolutely satisfied with your content. This is mind power through instant configuration.

Writing should be a habit that you practice constantly, especially for when you have those nerve-wracking moments and your brain suddenly freezes!

In conclusion, writing stimulates the mind and makes it work faster and more effectively. If you apply instant conditioning — snapping your brain to help you write — then concentration, speed, and quality will soon follow.

Chapter 5:

Testing Your Operating System

Exercise 1: Mapped Out Plans

Now, let's see if you can concentrate and focus your mind...

1.) What would a horizontal mind map look like for a satellite TV installer or technician?

2.) How would you set up your own horizontal mind map for mental numbness?

Try to apply this horizontal mind mapping for a week, and keep track of your improvement in terms of personal performance.

<u>Exercise</u> 2: Values Configuration

Work on the following table. Focus on the number **15** in the bottom right-hand corner to help you decide what numbers to put in the blank squares. Try to figure it out in *60 seconds*.

3	0			
	6			
		0		
	1		6	
6				15

ANSWER: *There is more than one solution to this puzzle; here is one of them:*

3	0	7	5	15
1	6	0	8	15
6	1	0	8	15
3	1	5	6	15
6	1	0	8	15

The first thing you should do when approaching this puzzle is ask yourself "what does this table tell me?"

This table tells you:

- When you add up the numbers diagonally (3 + 6 + 0 + 6), they equal 15. *This is the key to the whole puzzle.*

There isn't enough information provided horizontally and vertically, so start with the second diagonal of the table: 6 + 1 + 0 + ? = 15. The only number that can be in this space is 8.

If you have two boxes filled with the number 15, it's safe to assume that the other remaining boxes in that last column should also be filled with the number 15.

Now you can fill in the other spaces so that the horizontal rows add up to 15.

For example:

First row: 3 + 0 + 7 + 5 = 15

Second row: 1 + 6 + 0 + 8 = 15

Third row: 6 + 1 + 0 + 8 = 15

Fourth row: 3 + 1 + 5 + 6 = 15

Fifth row: 6 + 1 + 0 + 8 = 15

Now, how do you complete it in 60 seconds?

Because this is a tricky exercise, you must first identify the role of the number 15 in the bottom right-hand corner. Then, when you've finally understood how the table works, you can use the same combination of numbers in multiple rows, which will enable you to complete the table faster. For instance, in this table the combination 1 + 6 + 0 + 8 is used four times.

Exercise 3: Recorded Repetition Replay

Try the following experiment:

1.) Dress yourself up in a distinct way.

2.) Now, take mental notes on your outfit and write down the following:

"It is certain that the number 0 was only created after people realized that the abstract and the idea of emptiness were the beginning of all things.

3.) Read the sentence out loud. Then fold the piece of paper, put it in your pocket, and carry it with you for the rest of the day.

4.) On the next day, complete your assignment by wearing the same outfit. Concentrate on your outfit and try to remember the sentence you wrote down.

Exercise 4: Transfer Your Thoughts

To grasp immediate control over your thoughts, snap your brain through instant configuration and write about the following:

- Fashion

- A poem about your mom

- A sick note to your boss

(Remember, it's not always about being an expert on the topic, but rather it's more about how you present it.)

Exercise 5: Mentally Recording Your Process

WARM-UP:

Study the table below and arrange the dots so that there are only three dots in each row and in each column (wherever there is *at least* one dot, because some rows and columns will be empty.)

(Hint: There are only **three dots** that need to be moved once, either *horizontally* or *vertically,* to achieve this. Optimize your mind to work faster. You should be able to solve this puzzle in less than a minute.)

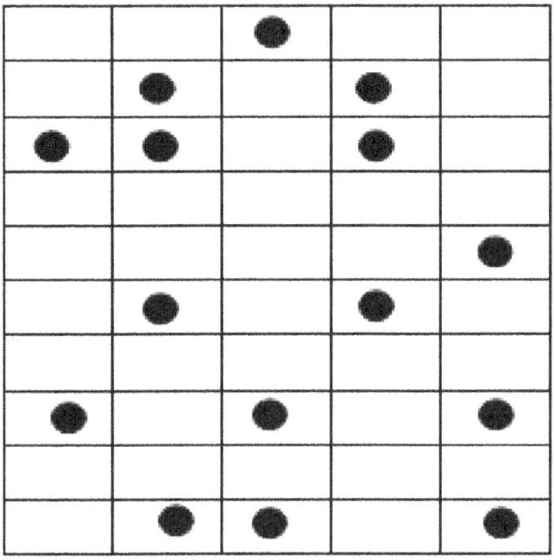

WARM-UP ANSWER:

(The three dots that only need to be moved once.)

Final Table:

	3	3	3	3	3
3		●	●	●	
3	●	●		●	
3	●			●	●
3	●		●		●
3		●	●		●

Only three dots are in each row and in each column.

REAL CHALLENGE:

Now that you're warmed up, try it again with the table below. This time you can horizontally or vertically move the dots as many times as you need to, as long as when you're finished there are only three dots per row and per column, with also no more than three dots diagonally. Think of it like solving a Rubik's cube.

Use the movie-scene repetition technique to recreate the same experience that produced your success in solving the warm-up puzzle. (Refresh yourself on the guidelines for this technique.)

You should be able to do this exercise quickly, increasing your speed every time (e.g., in 5 minutes, then 3, then 1). Train yourself as much as you can, so you can work faster each time.

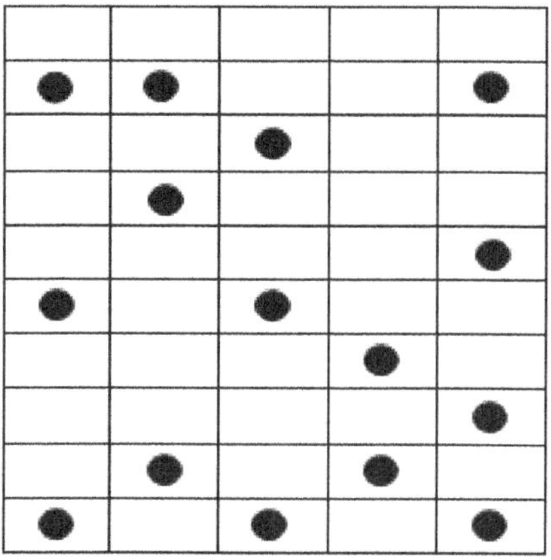

CHALLENGE ANSWER:

So, how do you work quickly on this table?

1.) First, move the dots up or down so that there are only three dots in each row horizontally.

2.) Then, count the dots diagonally and vertically.

3.) Finally, move any excess dots to the right and to the left so that you also have three dots aligned vertically, and do not have more than three dots joined diagonally.

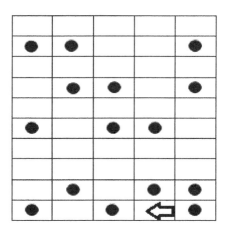

Final Table:

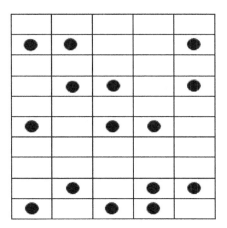

*There are many ways to align the dots in the correct pattern, but this method is the fastest.

Exercise 6: Pairing Compatibilities

Domino dancing   Ratatouille   Golden ages   Royal games

Religion   Mind games

1.) Observe the 6 cards above. Each card has a **symbol** or **illustration** on it. Each card also corresponds to a **phrase** or **word**.

2.) Look at the cards for *2 minutes* and memorize the **words** below each one of them.

3.) Cover the **words** with a ruler or a piece of paper. Quickly say each **word** or **phrase** that corresponds to each <u>card</u>.

4.) When you are done, cover the <u>cards</u> and quickly say which <u>card symbol</u> that corresponds to each **word** or **phrase**.

Which methodology did you use for this exercise?

<u>Exercise 7</u>: Processing Match

Try to identity the **number of identical banners** to the one <u>framed</u> (in the right corner) by using the following horizontal mind map:

- It has a squared centerpiece / It has an opening to the bottom / The center piece is a little bit upward compared to the wings.

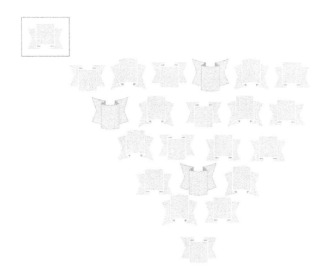

First, look at the framed picture for a moment, then concentrate on your mind mapping.

Then, find all the similar banners to the framed one in *15 seconds*. (Try as many times as you can until you are able to identify all of them in *15 seconds*).

Chapter 6:

System Upgrade Complete

Intelligence Comes In All Shapes And Sizes

"**Mind Power**" is not about being the smartest person in the room, but like any other normal and realizable personal goal, it can be attained by just about anybody.

People would be amazed to know how individually unique each person's mental prowess is.

You don't need to be "special" or a genius, you just need to do the right thing and follow the right steps and guidelines to become more alert and more capable.

There is no time like the present.

Final Review Logs

Follow these guidelines to get a better handle on your own mind power:

- Put yourself to work and create a pattern so that your mind can become more reactive.

- Test your mind's flexibility by conditioning it through writing.

- Use repetition the correct way (adopting the right moves and moving forward with them), so it can help you unleash your full mental potential.

- Numb your mind of all distraction for optimized focus so you can experience quicker results and effectiveness all the time.

So what are you waiting for? Don't just sit or stand there! It's time to "power up" your mind and boost your overall effectiveness!

An INSTANT Thank You!

Thank you for entrusting in the <u>INSTANT Series</u> to help you improve your life.

Our goal is simple, help you achieve instant results as fast as possible in the quickest amount of time. We hope we have done our job, and you have gotten a ton of value.

If you are in any way, shape, or form, dissatisfied, then please we encourage you to get refunded for your purchase because we only want our readers to be happy.

If, *on the other hand*, you've enjoyed it, if you can kindly leave us a review on where you have purchased this book, that would mean a lot.

What is there to do now?

Simple! Head over to http://www.instantseries.com, and sign up for our **newsletter** to stay up-to-date with the latest instant developments *(if you haven't done so already).*

Be sure to check other books in the INSTANT Series. If there is something you like to be added, be sure to let us know for as always we love your feedback.

Yes, we're on **social medias**. *Don't forget to follow us!*

https://www.facebook.com/InstantSeries

https://twitter.com/InstantSeries

https://plus.google.com/+Instantseries

Thank you, and wish you all the best!
- *The INSTANT Series Team*

Made in the USA
Monee, IL
04 February 2022

90591062R00039